The Ineffable Infinity

Whispers of the infinite!

Dr Niharika Yadav

BookLeaf Publishing

India | USA | UK

Made with ❤ on the BookLeaf Publishing Platform
www.bookleafpub.in
www.bookleafpub.com

Dedication

To Vihaan, my infinite light, and Google Junior, my ever-loyal companion—your love fills my world with joy.

To my mother, my unwavering pillar of strength; to my father and siblings, my tireless cheerleaders; to my husband, who nudges me toward growth every day; and to my friends, my guardian angels—I am because of you.

To everyone who has crossed paths with me and made me a better person for it—deep gratitude.

To the seekers, the wanderers, and the healers—may this book be a whisper of infinity, a reflection of the boundless journey of Shivatva.

With love and gratitude,
Dr Niharika

Preface

There are moments in life that words fail to capture—feelings too vast, emotions too deep, and experiences too profound. *"The Ineffable Infinity"* is my attempt to give voice to the unspoken, to paint the invisible, and to embrace the eternal within fleeting moments.

As a healer, I have realized that healing is not just about mending others—it is also about evolving within, breaking, learning, and rising again. In this journey of healing, I have found poetry to be my sanctuary, a place where I uncover the truths of my soul, one verse at a time.

This book is an ode to love, loss, hope, and the infinite possibilities of the universe. It is a reflection of my travels—both within and beyond—the friendships that have shaped me, the nature that nurtures me, and the unseen forces that guide me, motherhood that is my greatest blessing. May these words reach those who need them. May they be a mirror, a refuge, or simply a companion on your journey of infinite becoming.

With love and light!

Acknowledgements

With deep gratitude, I bow to the healers and gurus who have illuminated my path, guiding me toward wisdom, self-discovery, and the essence of seeking within. To my parents—my first teachers, my unwavering support, my foundation. My mother, my greatest strength, has shown me what resilience and unconditional love looks like. To my family—my siblings, my forever cheerleaders, whose laughter and encouragement uplift me, and my husband, who nudges me to be better every day—I am grateful for your love, patience, and belief in me.

To my son, Vihaan, my greatest blessing, and my dog, Google Junior, whose love knows no bounds—your presence fills my heart with infinite joy and purpose.

To my friends, my guardian angels—you have stood by me in moments of light and shadow, offering me love, kindness, and the courage to keep going. Life's journey would not have been as meaningful without you.

And to every soul who has touched my life, even in passing—thank you. You have been part of my healing, my evolution, and my infinite becoming.

10. I AM.. I AM INFINITE

I am that dew drop on the leaves,
I can glisten and quench your thirst.
The sun shines and helps me glisten in all glory,
And yet, it doesn't define me.
Be that sun, be the light that helps me shine,
But know—I will still glisten when clouds gather.
I will still be here, in the hush of dawn,
A quiet miracle, never truly gone.
I am...
I am infinite.

I am that wave in the sea,
I can be formidable, and yet, I can bring joy.
I emerge and ebb, the sea current helps me go on,
Yet the sea doesn't define me.
Be the sea that helps me rise after I ebb,
But know—I will return, unchained, untamed.
Even when I crash upon the shore,
I am not lost, I am forevermore.
I am...

I am infinite.

I am the cloud in the sky, clear and relentless,
I can be dark and angry, or soft as a whisper.
The day and night vary my shades,
Yet they don't define me.
Be the sky that lets me float,
That cradles my weight, yet never holds me still.
I am fleeting, I am eternal,
A shifting dream, a restless will.
I am...
I am infinite.

I am the fire in the ember's glow,
I flicker, I blaze, I smolder slow.
The wind may stir me, the rain may try,
Yet even in ashes, I do not die.
Be the breath that fuels my flame,
That fans my spark, yet sets me free.
For though I rise and though I fade,
I will always be—endlessly.
I am...
I am infinite.

2. SCENT OF A WOMAN

It's delicate, yet it's strong,
A whisper, a storm, a timeless song.
It's fierce and yet so gentle still,
A fire that warms, a will of steel.

It's resilient, yet tender to the touch,
Holding worlds, asking nothing much.
It's love that bends but never breaks,
Empathy that gives more than it takes.

It's gratitude woven with divinity,
A force beyond time, an infinity.
It's primal—wild, untamed, and free,
Yet ever-evolving, like tides in the sea.

It's forgiving, yet it won't forget,
A quiet strength, a whispered threat.
It's protective as the moonlit night,
Cradling life in hands of light.

It's vulnerable yet unafraid,
Unfolding truth, never swayed.
It's a force to reckon with, untamed,
Both fierce and soft, never framed.

It lingers, it stays, it marks the air,
A presence felt everywhere.
It's our essence, our fire, our grace,
It's the scent of a woman—time cannot erase.

3. THE DAWN AND DUSK OF CHARACTER

Imagine if colors only existed in black and white.

What if the days comprised just the day and night?

Would we really like to be deprived of the beautiful blend of dawn and dusk?

Without that beautiful transition, wouldn't our lives seem rushed and brusque?

Even the darkest night morphs into mesmerizing colors as it breaks into day,

It's that time when the skies defy the definition of time and have a unique story to convey.

Then why do we judge people and label them as just good or bad, period?

Didn't god create each human with tints and tones in a myriad?

Have we ever strived to live beyond just existing?

To love, seek, and evolve without resisting.

Look beyond, for there's more to you as a person,

We have all been created with the potential for
ambiversion.

Everyone is a sum-total of their life and just their day's
experience.
If only you look empathetically without judgment, you'll
see a confluence,
A confluence of greatness, the good, bad, and great
potential.
We can then see a true blend of human character, like
the dawn and dusk, that is quintessential.

4. MY WARMTH MY LIGHT!

You are the light that brightens my darkest days
You are my first thought in any phase...
You make my soul sing and my heart rejoice
You are my tranquility in all the noise.
You are the brightest color of life
You are all the goodness for which I strive.

My love, I always want you to remember
You're not alone, we can conquer the world together
I'll always be your silent cheerleader and your biggest
fan
I'll always be the strength for your journey from where
it began

When your dream seems distant and your mind is
exhausted
When you feel burdened and life seems twisted
When your heart doesn't feel so good
When you feel completely misunderstood

When everything seems hard and futile
When you want to give up just before that mile

My love, I always want you to remember
You're not alone, we can conquer the world together
I'll always be the silent cheerleader and your biggest fan
I'll always be the strength for your journey from where
it began

You are the river that flows and never stagnates
You are the heart that so much warmth radiates
You are the master of your destiny
You are the voice, and you are the remedy...
You are relentless and invincible
You are God's favorite miracle

My love, I always want you to remember
You're not alone, we can conquer the world together
I'll always be the silent cheerleader and your biggest fan
I'll always be the strength for your journey from where
it began

When things don't go your way
When your mind just wants to give up and sway...
When you're lost, and life doesn't treat you well,
Look back on this and on the good things your mind will
dwell

Because if I haven't said it enough
You have it in you to rise like the phoenix even where
it's tough

My love, I always want you to remember
You're not alone, we can conquer the world together
I'll always be the silent cheerleader and your biggest fan
I'll always be the strength for your journey from where
it began..

5. THE UNAPOLOGETIC MOTHER

I feel life stirring within me,
I wonder, I dream,
And with each passing day, I care a little less
about what the world expects of me.
I rise beyond the highest love I have ever known,
only to find there is still more to give.
This tiny stranger growing inside me—
fills me with wonder, fear, and a love so vast,
it defies explanation.
I am the unapologetic mother.

I cry over things as small as my coffee being too bitter,
or my reflection not shining as it once did.
I wrestle with clothes that no longer fit,
Watch my body transform in ways I never asked for,
yet I wear a smile,
for the little soul inside me feels every ounce of my
comfort.
I long for flavors unfamiliar,

or turn away from comforts I once cherished.
Some days, I feel like a goddess.
Some days, I feel like a stranger living in my body.

I am the unapologetic mother.
I choose to work until the moment my baby arrives,
or I choose to pause, to savor the time before we meet.
I embrace the waves of labor,
or I decide that science will guide the way.
I nurse him at my breast, cherishing the bond,
or I watch him thrive as a bottle feeds him with love.
I raise him to be the truest version of himself,
not the world's definition of who he should be.
I am the unapologetic mother.

I wrestle with guilt, glancing at my phone a hundred
times at work,
or I sit at home, wondering how far the world is moving
without me.
I rush home to judgmental stares after a long day,
or I stay back, unseen, as the weight of an unspoken
sacrifice lingers.
I battle expectations, my own and theirs,
yet I rise each day and do it all over again.
I am the unapologetic mother.

Perhaps I could judge less, love more—

extend a gentle smile to the mother lost in doubt.
For if God could not be everywhere,
He created mothers—flawed, yet infinite in strength.
No matter the path I take,
no day ever feels the same,
but every day, I give all of me and then some,
Because I am, and always will be,
"The unapologetic mother"

6. FOOTPRINTS ON WATER

I am the river, ever flowing and fluid, never still,
A flowing song and ode to all who have touched my
soul.
Their whispers dissolve into my currents,
Their touch leaves nothing behind but **footprints on
water.**

I have borne laughter like sunlight on my waves,
and sorrow that sank deep into my depths.
Some linger as whirlpools, pulling me back,
Yet they fade away like **footprints on water.**

Impermanence is my name, yet I remember,
Not in stillness, but in the way I flow.
For though I wash away all in my path, I also carry—
Echoes of love in **footprints on water.**

I have kissed the earth, carved my way through depths,
Yet I do not belong to where I've been.

No matter how much I embrace the land,
I leave only fleeting **footprints on water**.

I have lost track of where I began,
But in my journey, I quenched countless souls.
I am stillness, the ripples and whirlpools,
A credence **footprints on water**.

And when I finally meet the ocean,
Will I disappear, or will I become whole?
Even as I surrender and become one with something
greater,
I will still carry **footprints on water**-
for I am not the echoes that fade, but the tide that
endures.

7. IF THE NINE YARDS COULD SPEAK

If the nine yards could speak,
they would whisper tales spun from love's tender thread
—

a story stitched with grace,
woven with strength and vulnerability,
like a dance of fire and water,
each fold carrying its own weight, its own truth.

As a child, I sat in awe,
my gaze fixed on my mother,
her hands moving with reverence,
as the fabric fell around her like a waterfall,
transforming her, not that she wasn't already a vision,
but something about the nine-yards
made her seem more than mortal,
more than human—
a goddess draped in the essence of womanhood.
They whispered of power,
of resilience, of the quiet strength

that rises from deep within,
and I, wide-eyed, longed to wear it,
to feel the weight of her strength,
to be wrapped in the stories of those who came before.

Through the years, I watched the women of my life—
mothers, aunts, grandmothers—
wrap themselves in dignity,
their presence unspoken, yet undeniable,
each pleat a testament to a life lived,
each drape a symbol of grace.
But time, relentless in its march,
shifted the nine yards from the essence of an Indian
woman
to something rare, something saved for moments
that seemed to slip away like grains of sand,
and sometimes, not even that.
I once swore I'd never drape it,
the fabric too much, too intricate,
too much to manage, too much to carry.

It was that "one day", I wrapped myself in it,
for a wedding, for a memory,
and with every pleat that fell into place,
I was transported—
back to the stories, back to the women,
to the strength I had always known,

but had never truly felt.

For the first time, I stood not just as a woman,
but as *the* woman—
the one who commands attention with grace,
who wears her confidence like a second skin,
who knows she is meant to be seen, to be revered.
And in that moment, I understood—
there is no feeling quite like it,
no other garment can summon such power.

If the nine yards could speak,
they would tell you of the infinite stories they carry—
they see no size, no shape, no color,
only the heart that wears them,
the soul that holds them close.
They tell the stories of homes and hearts,
woven into every thread,
whispering of the essence of womanhood,
unbroken, unyielding, everlasting.

If only the nine yards could speak,
they would sing of the heart of every house,
the soul of every woman,
the quiet strength found in every fold,
every pleat, every turn.
They are not just fabric—

they are living memories,
a tapestry of all that has been and all that will be,
woven together in the silent language of love,
draped across time and tradition.

If only the nine yards could speak..

8. ME BEFORE YOU

I have a distant memory of someone I used to know
She was carefree, a mix of laughter and tears; she always
went with the flow
I try to remember who I was before I became a reflection
of your energy
The woman who emptied her cup and poured the last
drop and became the synergy
I wonder who I was before you, the me before you.

Did I live for myself, did I know what truly
unconditional love meant?
Did I know the elixir of true love, did I ever feel the
torment?
I try to look back and I see a faint shadow, a woman who
lived for today
Being full of energy a woman who was just a girl,
daughter, and bae
I wonder who I was before you, the me before you.

Was I truly happy, did I ever really live or was it just

existing?
Was I the version of me I am today or was I just drifting?
I see a woman full of energy, panache, and gumption,
Did it just get stronger with the fierce sense of need for
protection
I wonder who I was before you, the me before you.

With you in my arms, did the flame in me turn into a
fire?
Did I become whole with the fulfillment of my heart's
desire?
Did my face gain some lines and my smile gain true
depth?
Did I finally find the door where the key to my
happiness was kept?
I wonder who I was before you, the me before you.

Was I that puzzle with a missing piece
Me after you; is that where my discontent begins to ease,
Sometimes I dream of visiting you in a parallel universe
just the way I was
I wonder if you'd still see me as the moon, and gravitate
to me with all my flaws
I wonder who I was before you, the me before you.

9. THE SACRED FUSION

In twilight's whispered hush, where night dissolves in
dawn,
A sacred dance awakens, two souls in union drawn.
The Ardha-Nareshwara's embrace, a rhythm deep and
true,
Within each heart's still chamber, this harmony shines
through.

O Shakti, wild and fierce, a tempest on the sea,
Your fire lights the spirit, your passion sets it free.
A force untamed, electric, the cosmos bows in awe,
A blazing star of power, the pulse in nature's law.

You dance upon the cosmos, in footsteps bold and bright,
With every step creation sings, the stars absorb your
light.
In thunder's voice, in rivers wild, in petals kissed by air,
Your presence hums in whispers deep, in fire, and in
prayer.

And Shiva, vast and silent, the mountain's steadfast
grace,
In stillness, worlds find refuge, in calm, their rightful
place.
Like rivers carving wisdom through time's eternal
stream,
You hold the sky in quiet strength, the guardian of the
dream.

Your breath is wind, your gaze the stars, your touch the
flowing tide,
In meditative silence, where endless truths reside.
A crescent moon upon your brow, a third eye full of
sight,
The universe within your mind, both shadow and pure
light.

Together they entwine, the dance of dusk and light,
A heart full of completeness, of shadow, and of sight.
In love, they forge the cosmos, in balance, life unfolds,
The Ardhanarishvara's blessing—a truth the spirit holds.

In every pulse of mortal hearts, their echoes intertwine,
A perfect blend of strength and grace, a force both fierce,
divine.
The fire that dares, the calm that soothes, the silence, and
the song,

The rhythm of existence, where both have danced so
long.

So let them rise within us, the fierce and gentle flame,
To walk the path of balance, where all is one, the same.
For in the soul's deep silence, where Shakti and Shiv
reside,
We find the perfect harmony, where truth and love abide.

1. THE ROAD TO ME

I walked a road of doubt and pain,
Through years of loss, through love, through rain.
I held regrets like autumn leaves,
Clutched tight within my folded sleeves.

I did not know, I could not see,
The weight of what was asked of me.
Yet still, I stood, I fell, I rose,
And bore my burdens as they chose.

I forgive the hands that shaped my way,
The ones who tore, who did not stay.
I let them go like drifting snow,
No longer mine to grasp or know.

I pardon time for moving fast,
For making moments fade into the past.
For lessons learned too late, too slow,
For roads not walked, for seeds that won't grow.

And most of all, my heart, be free—
I grant forgiveness now to "me".
For anger kept, for words unsaid,
For nights where doubt still made its bed.

But love, I vow, shall take its place,
No lesser light, no fleeting grace.
I see myself beyond the name,
Beyond the roles, beyond the frame.

Not only daughter, mother, wife,
Not only bound by work or life.
I am the earth, the wind, the sea,
A spark within eternity.

I take my flaws, I make them mine,
A thread within the grand design.
Each day, I wake to something new,
Another step, another view.

And when I reach some distant hill,
I'll turn to see the journey still—
Not with regret, nor fear, nor blame,
But as a soul who dared to claim.

11. THE SILENCE BETWEEEN WORDS

There is a silence between words,
a hush where the heart folds its wings,
where the tongue surrenders its weapons
and the mind kneels before something greater.

I have held words like stones in my mouth,
ready to build or to break,
to shape walls of sorrow or bridges of fire.
But silence—ah, silence—
it lingers like an ocean before the storm,
a pause heavy with unspoken thunder.

I have seen silence slip between lovers,
thick as a night without moonlight,
where fingers tremble,
searching for a language no lips can form.
A silence that burns like a slow-setting sun,
a farewell carved into the marrow of time.

I have wielded silence as a dagger,
letting absence carve its deep, cold lines,
watching it settle into wounds like winter frost.
And I have offered it as a balm,
a breath between sorrows,
a prayer that needed no sound to be heard.

I have heard silence in the breaking of waves,
in the hush of snowfall blanketing a forgotten city,
in the last glance of a friend before parting,
where no word can hold what the eyes already know.

Silence is the marrow of longing,
the echo of the universe before it spoke,
the space where truth lingers,
too sacred to be caged in syllables.

Let me wear my silence like a cloak,
woven with midnight and fireflies,
where words are no longer prisons,
but birds that know when to sing
and when to rest in the sky.

For silence is not emptiness—
it is the essence of something greater,
a love so vast it does not need a name,

a presence so whole it can only be felt,
like the weight of the stars pressing softly on my skin.

12. THE LAST TRAIN HOME

The platform hums with quiet goodbyes,
the scent of rain on iron tracks,
the weight of time pressed into the soles of my shoes.
I have carried the past in a tattered suitcase,
worn at the edges, heavy with names
I no longer call in the dark.

The whistle cries—a thin, spectral voice—
a sound neither here nor there,
a note stretched between arrival and departure.
And so I step forward, not knowing if I leave or return,
if the rails bend toward exile or embrace.

What was it I held so tightly?
A love that unraveled like thread in my hands,
a road not taken but traced in thought,
a sorrow polished smooth by time?
The past lingers, but only as mist—
it does not board this train.

The journey is neither escape nor pursuit,
only motion, only the rhythm of steel and breath.
The carriage rocks like a lullaby
for the uncertain, the in-between,
for those who have outgrown yesterday
but have not yet learned the shape of tomorrow.

The train's pulse quickens;
it calls me forward into the unknown,
where silence is no longer emptiness,
but a place for the heart to rest,
for the mind to release its grip on old wounds.
Each turn of the wheel is an invitation,
a promise made to those who dare not look back.

Outside, the world flickers past—
a blur of rooftops, of rivers, of nameless fields,
each one a story I might have lived.
And yet, I do not grieve for them.
The unknown stretches ahead, vast and unbeaten,
not a void, but a canvas waiting for my touch.
I am not running from the past,
but walking with it, side by side,
until it becomes part of the air I breathe,
and the horizon becomes my own.

The train does not wait for those who hesitate.
It does not offer farewells,
only the rustling of leaves and the steady pulse of life,
reminding me that time does not demand permission.
I have known the pain of endings,
but I have learned the grace of beginnings.

There is no fear in departure,
only the quiet understanding that every station,
no matter how distant,
has always been a part of home.
I leave no part of me behind,
but carry it with me—woven into the rhythm of the
train,
each moment a thread that stitches me to the future,
each second a stitch unraveling the past.

And when the whistle calls again,
I will not look back,
for the destination has already arrived
in the very act of leaving.

13. THE LIGHT THAT FILLS ME

I wake with the hush of dawn,
light spilling like quiet forgiveness through my window.
The world breathes, and so do I.
Not perfect, not untouched,
but here—whole in the ways that matter.

I have known pain,
worn its name like a threadbare coat,
felt the weight of absence,
the silence of things unspoken.
But today, I count what remains.

The hands that held me,
even when I did not ask.
The voices that called me back to myself,
when I wandered too far into my own storms.
The love that stayed,
not always loud, not always in sight,
but steady as the earth beneath my feet.

Gratitude is not a grand thing—
not a prayer shouted to the sky,
not a debt to be repaid.
It is a whisper in the bones,
a quiet knowing that I am held,
even when I stand alone.

So I gather it gently,
like fallen petals after rain,
and let it shape me,
soften me,
fill the spaces where sorrow once lived.
For every lesson,
for every loss,
for every day I wake anew—

I say, **thank you.**

14. A RENDEZVOUS WITH MY YOUNGER SELF

She was waiting for me, barefoot on the edge of memory,
eyes wide with wonder, heart untamed,
the younger me—too full of questions,
too tangled in the weight of things she could not name.

She studied me, arms crossed,
measuring the years between us,
searching for traces of herself in my face.
"Did we make it?" she asked,
not with hope, but with hesitation.
"How did we get here? To this place of peace,
of forgiveness, of gratitude?"

I did not answer right away.
She had more to say, and I owed her the space to say it.

She talked about the unrest in her life,
how she became the quiet while drowning in noise,
how high emotions raged around her like storms,

but silence sat heavy when the storms passed.
She had been a bridge, always a bridge—
carrying the weight of others,
afraid to crumble, afraid to fall.

She talked about the worry—
of being enough, of fulfilling a dream
that was never truly hers, but her mother's.
The pressure of a title, a role, a duty.
Doctor. Healer. Fixer of broken things.
But who would fix her?

She talked about clinging too tightly
to anyone who cared, anyone who stayed.
Afraid that if she let go, she'd disappear.
She talked about the mirror,
the battle between what she saw and what she felt.
The body she never fully called her own.
The weight of expectation pressing into her skin.

She talked about always doing the right thing,
because she didn't know who she was without it.
She talked about **existing**
when all she wanted was to **live.**

She took a breath then,
her hands twisting together, waiting for my answer.

I reached for them—
small fingers still soft with uncertainty,
still reaching for something solid.

"We got here slowly," I told her.
"One day at a time, one breath at a time.
Not through winning, not through perfection,
but by learning when to hold on and when to let go."

"I let go of the noise that wasn't mine to carry.
I let go of the guilt of choosing myself.
I let go of the fear of not being enough,
because I am not just a daughter, not just a doctor,
not just what the world expects me to be.
I am more."

I told her that peace wasn't something I found—
it was something I built.
Brick by brick, tear by tear,
forgiving the world, forgiving myself,
learning that love is not a lifeline, but a gift.

And I told her,
"You don't have to prove yourself.
You don't have to be the bridge if you don't want to.
You are allowed to just **be.**"

She blinked at me,
the tension in her shoulders easing just a little.
And then, she smiled.
Not the one she wore for the world,
but a real one—mine.

And just like that,
she ran off into the past,
and I walked forward into tomorrow,
lighter than before.

15. THE WEIGHT OF A SHOOTING STAR

They said, **"Chase your dreams."**
So I did—
barefoot and breathless,
with nothing but hunger in my hands
and stardust in my lungs.

But they never spoke of the toll.

They never said ambition is a gluttonous thing,
devouring time, swallowing ease,
leaving behind an appetite that never quiets.
That it steals the softness from sleep,
replaces it with lists carved into the skull—
a mind that refuses to yield,
a heart that pounds like a knocking fist.

They never warned me
that a woman who reaches too high
is seen as both spectacle and storm.

That every worspace is an arena,
every idea a test,
every confident stride a reason for whispers.

They never told me that ambition
doesn't just demand sacrifice—
it **is** the sacrifice.
It is conflict between birthdays and deadlines,
meals eaten standing,
friends left waiting in unread messages.

It is learning to love from a distance,
to stand at the edge of your own life,
watching it unfold like a play
where you are both the lead
and the missing character.

And yet—
I **do not regret it.**

Because the ache of longing
is still softer
than the weight of a dream buried alive.
So I let the hunger stay.
I let it drive me forward,
because I have made peace
with the price I pay.

16. THE GLASS SKIN

I have spent years learning to be porcelain,
to let the light reflect off me,
to smile in a way that reassures—
a surface too smooth to question,
too polished to break.

I have worn silence like silk,
draped it over my bones,
let it keep me from shattering.
Because a woman who bends but never breaks
is easier to admire.
A woman who absorbs, who absorbs, who absorbs—
but never spills—
is easier to love.

But I know the truth.
Glass does not crack without warning.
It holds, it flexes,
until one day—
a pressure too sharp, a touch too heavy,

and suddenly—pieces.

Some days, I feel the fractures beneath,
the splintering of "should-haves" and "must-bes",
the fault lines of expectation running through me.
I am told to be soft, but not weak.
Strong, but not intimidating.
Ambitious, but humble.
Brilliant, but quiet about it.

I walk this tightrope
between **too much and not enough,**
between who they expect
and who I long to be.

But today, I run my fingers over the cracks,
marvel at how the light catches in them,
how they glow like gold beneath the weight of morning.

Maybe breaking is not the end.
Maybe glass, when shattered,
is just waiting to be remade—
into something jagged, something beautiful,
something that still catches the sun.

17. SCARLET STATEMENTS

Some mornings, I wake up fragile—
a feather caught in the breath of the world,
a shadow that barely clings to its shape.

But I do not stay this way.
I reach for the bullet of red,
twist it up like a soldier arming herself,
drag its defiance across my lips.

It is not just pigment,
not just vanity,
but **alchemy.**

It pulls the spine straighter,
sharpening my edges,
painting over doubt with something bolder,
something that refuses to be ignored.

They call it **"too much."**

Too loud. Too bright. Too bold.
But have they ever watched a woman
color herself fearless?
Have they ever seen how a shade of crimson
turns silence into statement?

They will not name me delicate today.
They will not mistake my softness for surrender.
This war paint is not for them,
it is for **me.**

A declaration in carmine:
I am here. I will not shrink.

So let them call it unnecessary.
Let them call it a mask.
They do not know what it means
to **reclaim yourself**
with nothing but a mirror
and a shade that burns like fire.

18. THE FOOTPRINTS WE LEAVE BEHIND

I do not walk this earth alone.
The wind hums my mother's song,
the soil cradles my father's bones,
and every step I take—
is a story pressed into the dust.

I leave behind more than footprints.
I leave behind the laughter that lingers in rooms
long after I have left.
I leave behind love woven into warm embraces,
whispers tucked into the folds of old letters,
promises I meant and did not break.

I leave behind scars, too—
the kind that teaches, the kind that burns,
the kind that prove I lived.
I leave behind quiet battles fought in silence,
the late-night tears no one ever saw,
the strength that rose from the ruins.

And when I go,
when my name is only a memory,
may the earth still carry
the echoes of my kindness,
the weight of my words,
the strength of my fire.

Let my footprints be more than marks in the dust—
let them be seeds,
let them be maps,
let them be the proof
that I **was here.**

And if one day, a weary traveler
should find my footprints on their road,
may they know they are not alone,
may they know someone walked this path before,
may they know, even in my absence,
I am with them.

19. THE SPACES BETWEEN THE SECONDS

There is a moment—
before the door swings open,
before the last train leaves,
before the sky collapses into dusk—
where time folds into itself.

It is the space between the seconds,
where regret hums like an old clock,
where footsteps of the past
presses lightly on the present,
where voices—once sharp, once clear—
soften into echoes
we barely recognize.

Did I hold enough hands?
Did I leave my words in the right places?
Did I love as much as I should have?
Or did I simply exist,
floating between faces and days,

never truly belonging
to any of them?

But time does not answer.
It does not pause.
It only moves—forward, forward—
like the tide that forgets the shore
it once kissed so tenderly.

And so I step into tomorrow,
knowing that every moment lost
was once a moment held—
and perhaps that is enough.
Yet sometimes, in the hush of midnight,

I reach into those spaces,
those seconds left behind,
pulling at the threads of what was almost said,
what was almost done,
what was almost changed.

I watch the past flicker in candlelight,
faces blurring at the edges,
laughter half-remembered,
grief pressing its palms against the glass.

And still, the train moves forward.

The station vanishes behind me.
I sit with my hands in my lap,
no longer clenching, no longer reaching,
but resting.

Because I have learned—
the past does not hold me.
I am not trapped in the spaces between.
I am here. I am moving. I am free.

20. THE WOMAN WHO CARRIES THE SKY

She walks with the weight of old prayers,
carrying the voices of the women before her—
the ones who whispered, the ones who wept,
the ones who dreamed with open eyes.

She is built of all her yesterdays,
stitched together by sorrow and survival,
braided with joy, laced with longing,
woven from fire and quiet resilience.

She does not break; she bends.
She does not beg; she rises.
She does not ask the world to make space for her—
she takes it, carves it,
shapes it into something new, something hers.

There was a time she doubted—
a time she believed she was too much,
too loud, too soft, too unfinished.

A time she measured herself
by the weight of others' words,
by the space she took up,
by the love she gave
but never kept for herself.

She remembers the girl she was—
clinging to approval like a lifeline,
carrying burdens that were never hers to hold,
taught to shrink, to wait, to endure.

But she has learned:
there is no such thing as too much
for a woman who carries the sky.
She is the storm and the stillness.
The root and the bloom.
The past and the possibility.

She is the woman she once feared becoming.
And oh, how beautiful she is.

Because now, when she speaks,
her voice does not waver.
Now, when she loves,
she does not hesitate.
Now, when she walks,
she leaves footprints made of fire.

She does not just exist—
she is a woman who carries the sky.

21. THE SHADOWS OF THE ROADS UNTAKEN

There are houses I have never entered,
yet their doors remain ajar.
There are names I have never spoken,
yet they shine like distant stars.

There are roads I did not wander,
forks where I turned away—
and in the hush between my footsteps,
I hear the ghosts of yesterday.

The child I never cradled,
the love I did not chase,
the letters left unwritten,
the hands I failed to trace.

Do they linger in the ether,
those moments never claimed?
Do they whisper through the keyholes
of the doors that stayed unnamed?

I see them in the mirror's fog—
a life that might have been.
A woman standing taller,
a girl still lost within.

Yet I do not reach to hold them,
nor beg for time to bend,
for I have learned that even echoes
fade gently in the end.

The roads I chose were never wrong,
the paths I walked were true,
for even shadows not yet cast
belong to me, to you.

And what of all the songs unsung,
the dreams I left behind?
They rise like mist at the break of dawn,
then slip beyond my mind.

For every door I left unopened,
another took its place.
For every love I could have known,
a different touch, a different face.

So let them shine like distant stars,

let them wander past my sight—
for the life I live, the steps I take,
are **mine**—and they are right.